DO TRY THIS AT HOME!

The Punk Science team live and work in the Science Museum. They spend their days performing experiments of all shapes and sizes and on the odd occasion performing science shows.

The Punk Scientists are Jon Milton, the fearless and clueless leader of the team. He's always ready with a plan – it's not always a good one, but it is a plan nonetheless. He likes experiments that help him with his hobbies of flying and scuba diving. By hobbies we actually mean things he'd like to do if he wasn't so lazy.

Brad Gross is the number-one American on the Punk Science team, and that has nothing to do with him being the only American on the Punk Science team. When Brad isn't doing experiments he's drumming, and when he's not drumming he's talking, and when he's not talking he's experimenting, and when he's not experimenting he's drumming, and so on; it's very much a drum, talk, experiment cycle. Brad is living proof that science isn't just for clever people.

Last and certainly not least is Dan Carter Hope. In Dan's head he is the ultimate guitar-playing action hero. Unfortunately for him, his action-hero status doesn't go any further than his head. Not even a little bit into his neck. However, his guitar playing does stretch a little further, although it seems to fall short of his fingers. This doesn't stop him from performing exciting experiments; it just makes it really difficult to see what he's doing because most of the time he's too afraid to look.

Macmillan Children's Books is delighted to be publishing the following brilliant books in association with the Science Museum

Why Is Snot Green?
And other extremely important questions (and answers)
from the Science Museum
Glenn Murphy

How Loud Can You Burp?
And other extremely important questions (and answers)
from the Science Museum
Glenn Murphy

Stuff That Scares Your Pants Off!
The Science Museum Book of Scary Things
(and how to avoid them)
Glenn Murphy

Your Planet Needs You!
A Kids' Guide to Going Green
Dave Reay

DO TRY THIS AT HOME!

28 spectacular experiments for scientists of all ages

Jon Milton

Illustrated by Mike Phillips

Photography by Jennie Hills

MACMILLAN CHILDREN'S BOOKS

Thanks to Deborah Bloxam, Gaby Morgan, the Institute of Physics, Claire Tomkin, Matthew Sommerich, Dan Albert, Alison Boyle, Peter Morris, Annie Devitt, Matt Moore, Nicola (for putting up with the mess I made at home) and Milo – J.M.

First published 2008 by Macmillan Children's Books

This edition published 2010 by Macmillan Children's Books
a division of Macmillan Publishers Limited
20 New Wharf Road, London N1 9RR
Basingstoke and Oxford
Associated companies throughout the world
www.panmacmillan.com

ISBN 978-0-330-50806-3

1 3 5 7 9 8 6 4 2

A CIP catalogue record for this book is available from
the British Library.

Printed and bound in China

Contents

Introduction

Doing experiments is great! It's one of the best things about science, testing stuff out to show how and why everything works. The three of us at Punk Science HQ at the Science Museum love doing experiments and we wanted to show you how to do them too. Some are quite easy and some are a bit more tricky. Don't worry though – we'll show you all the stuff you need and what to do with it. There are even plenty of pictures of us actually doing the experiments, showing that we haven't cheated and that they really work.

We've got six different sections. Flight & Space, where we'll show you how to make flying things and why they fly. If you're not too tired from all that flapping about, you should have enough energy left for the, err . . . Energy chapter. Electricity & Magnetism is all about sparks and attraction – no, it's not about romance, it's cool experiments. We've got pushes and pulls in the Forces section. In Light & Sound you'll be able to do weird things with what you see and what you hear. And finally a chapter bubbling with experiments all about Chemistry, where you'll get to mix some concoctions and make reactions. There are going to be a couple of tricky scientific words along the way, like dribble and fluff (actually they're not very scientific at all). But for any words that are tricky there is a rather handy glossary at the back of the book. That's not the only great thing at the back of the book – there's also the most awesome quiz the world has ever seen. Well, maybe not the 'world has ever seen', but definitely the most awesome that you'll see at the exact moment you look at it.

What are you waiting for? You need to start experimenting . . . Go on then . . . Why are you still reading this bit? . . . Turn the page and get started . . . Seriously, nothing else is going to happen on this page . . . Right, fine! Stay on this page if that's what you want . . . But stay here on your own, because we're off to the next page . . . See ya!

Flight & Space

Birds think they're better than us because they can fly, but anything a bird can do we humans can do better.

Or so you'd think, but it turns out flying is actually quite hard to do. It's all well and good trying to copy birds by flapping your arms, but it won't get you off the ground. Humans don't have the necessary equipment. That's why people went about making clever things to help us fly. Lots of people just stuck feathers on their arms, which is not only rubbish but makes you look really silly – and, besides, you don't want to copy birds too much, otherwise we'll be living in nests and laying eggs before we know it.

So it was lucky that the first successful bit of flying didn't involve wings at all. Back in 1783 two French brothers, Joseph and Etienne Montgolfier, made the first hot-air balloon that could carry people. To honour that achievement we're going to have a go at making our own balloon later on in this chapter.

When we think of flight, we usually think of two pioneers: the Wright brothers.

The Wright brothers were the first people to do controlled powered flight, just like the planes that you see in the sky. Except that they only flew for 12 seconds and their plane was made out of bicycle parts, which doesn't sound great, but it was ages ago in 1903 and they did stay up for a bit longer later on.

Flying is hard, especially having control of where you're going. There are four big things you have to deal with: Lift, Gravity, Thrust and Drag. Lift makes you go up, gravity pulls you down, thrust moves you forward and drag slows you down. Lift and gravity work against each other and so do thrust and drag. You have to balance all four in order to fly.

How do you get a baby astronaut to sleep?

Rock it

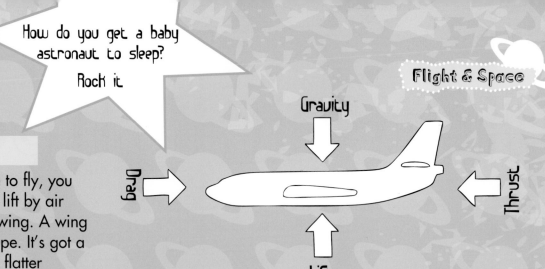

Gravity

Drag

Thrust

Lift

Lift

For an aeroplane to fly, you need lift. You get lift by air flowing over the wing. A wing is an aerofoil shape. It's got a curved top and a flatter bottom. Air moves faster over the top of the wing than under it, creating lower pressure above the wing than below it. This is what creates lift.

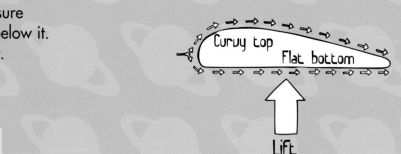

Curvy top

Flat bottom

Lift

Thrust

Thrust is created by propellers or by jet engines. These push the plane forward, creating the airflow over the wing.

Drag

Drag is a bit of a drag. It slows you down when you want to go fast. Planes need to be streamlined to keep drag to a minimum.

Gravity

Gravity does what it always does. It's a force that pulls things together – in this case, our plane to the Earth.

Flying is good, but flying into space is better. Like the Punk Scientists we are, we've often dreamed of going further than just flying around the Earth. We want to go higher; we want to go into space. Other people have been there – in fact there was a bit of competition between Russia and the USA in the 1960s when manned space travel was getting started. Russia got up there first but the USA made it to the moon first, so we'll call it a draw.

We said flying was hard, but flying into space is even harder. You need more power, more fuel and once you're in space you need to be able to cope without air and in reduced gravity. We can't show you how to make a real spacecraft, but in this chapter we can show you how they work.

Hot-air Balloon

If something is lighter than air it tends to want to float upwards. That's why gases that are lighter than air, like helium, are put in balloons. You don't need special gas to make our floating balloon, just some hot air. But not the sort of hot air that comes out of Brad's mouth – that's just boring and a little bit smelly.

Let's start making it.

You'll need:
- 4 sheets of tissue paper
- Scissors
- Glue
- 4 paper clips
- A hairdryer

1. Got all that? Good. Because we're getting started. We've taken the tissue paper and folded it in half. Be careful not to get a paper cut – ouch, that stings.

2. Cut along the unfolded side to make curved edges.

3. Take each curved edge and glue it to another sheet's curved edge, until they are all completely joined with a gap in the bottom only.

Don't glue it like this!

5. Put the hairdryer underneath the balloon and blow hot air into it. The balloon will fill up with hot air and will float upwards.

What's happening?

This works because hot air is quite clever stuff. The hot air inside the balloon becomes less dense than the cool air outside the balloon. It's this difference that makes the balloon rise.

4. Wait for the glue to dry and then carefully open up the balloon so you can fill it with air. Attach the paper clips to the bottom of the balloon to give it a little bit of weight.

RATINGS

Difficulty
✈ ✈ ✈ ✈
You'll need to be pretty accurate.

Messy
✈ ✈ ✈ ✈
You might get stuck on a couple of bits . . . of paper.

Grown-up helper
✈ ✈ ✈ ✈
You might need some help with the cutting or sticking.

Time ⏱
This should take you about **30 minutes**, which includes time for the glue to dry.

Helicopter

We at Punk Science love helicopters, but Jon loves them the most. Jon says, 'One day I want to be a helicopter . . . I mean a helicopter pilot.'

Here's how to make a mini helicopter.

You'll need:
- 2 pencils
- Sticky tape
- Scissors
- 2 pieces of card
- Glue

1. Take the two pencils and tape them together to make a 'T' shape.

2. Cut two strips of card.

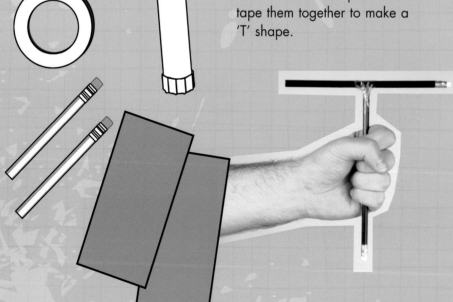

RATINGS

Difficulty
✈ ✈ ✈ ✈ ✈
If you don't get it right, it'll crash.

Messy
✈ ✈ ✈ ✈ ✈
It's not at all messy unless you get stuck to the sticky tape, so just don't.

Grown-up helper
✈ ✈ ✈ ✈ ✈
You might need some help with the cutting.

Time ⏱
This should take you about **10** minutes.

3. Fold the card over so each piece makes the shape of an aerofoil (curved on the top, flatter on the bottom, like we saw at the start of the chapter). Do this by gluing the ends down so they look like teardrops. But don't start crying to see what teardrops look like – just look at the picture.

Use a bit of tape to stick the aerofoils to the pencils. Make sure they are pointing in opposite directions.

4. It works really well, but the higher you drop it from the better it works. Not too high though, as you might fall down and hurt yourself. It's also a smart move to check that you have a safe landing zone as well. It'll spin down to the ground.

What's a pilot's favourite flavour of crisps?
Plane.

What's happening?

There is a slight flaw in our helicopter that makes it ever so slightly inferior to a real helicopter. Where a real helicopter can take off and land vertically, the Punk Science helicopter only really lands vertically. In fact, it doesn't take off at all because it's dropped. A real helicopter cheats by using an engine to turn the rotor blades so it can take off. The helicopter blades are spun through the air to create lift.

Hovercraft

DO THIS AT TRY HOME!

It may not fly high, but it does hover a bit above the ground and that's good enough for us. It's a hovercraft and they are lots of fun, almost as much fun as eating ice cream. So we thought we'd combine the two and make an ice-cream hovercraft, but it melted. So instead we thought we'd use the ice-cream tub to make the hovercraft, but it does mean eating all the ice cream first. Oh well, if we have to.

Here's how to make a hovercraft.

GROWN-UP HELPER NEEDED!

1. Place the nozzle of the hairdryer on the outside of the bottom of the tub and draw around it using the marker pen. Cut the circle out. Be careful – you might need an adult to help you.

2. Put the hairdryer far enough into the hole so it stays put.

You'll need:
- A hairdryer
- An empty ice-cream tub
- A marker pen
- Scissors

RATINGS

Difficulty
✈ ✈ ✈ ✈ ✈
Get this wrong and you don't deserve to be a punk scientist.

Messy
✈ ✈ ✈ ✈ ✈
No mess, no fuss, just hovering.

Grown-up helper
✈ ✈ ✈ ✈ ✈
An adult will probably need to cut the hole in the ice-cream tub and help you turn the hairdryer on and off.

Time 🕐
This should take you about **10 minutes**.

3. Switch the hairdryer on – it's hover time! We've decorated ours so it looks a bit more like a hovercraft. You can do the same, but don't let Brad do it as it'll look as rubbish as ours does.

What's happening?

Like a real hovercraft, our ice-cream tub is hovering on a cushion of air. We made this cushion of air by turning the hairdryer on. It pushes air down into the tub, but the air hasn't got anywhere to go so it escapes out of the bottom, lifting the ice-cream tub up. Hovercrafts work best on flat surfaces, because too many lumps and bumps disrupt the way the air comes out of the bottom and they don't hover so well.

FACT

Have you ever thought how great it is lazing in bed and then thought how great flying is and then thought, Wouldn't it be great to be able to do both at the same time? No? Just us then. Amazingly, it has been done. In 1954 the flying bedstead took off. It wasn't actually a bed – it was a jet engine on a frame that looked like a bed, but it could do vertical take-offs and was the fore-runner of the Harrier jet.

Bernoulli Ball

DO THIS AT TRY HOME!

Have you ever wondered how you could use a straw to demonstrate the theory of lift? What do you mean, no? We're thinking about it all the time. In fact, we're thinking about it at this very instant, on this page, right now.
I wonder if I could use this straw to fly? No, a straw can't be used to a make a person fly – that would be as stupid as having trousers made of coconuts.
But a straw *can* be used to make a lightweight ball fly.

GROWN-UP HELPER NEEDED!

Let's demonstrate the theory of lift.

You'll need:
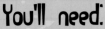
- A lightweight ball
- A straw
- A hairdryer

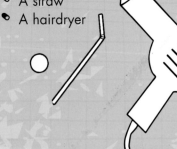

1. Hold the ball above the straw and blow as hard as you can.

2.
You can see the ball is hovering above the straw. You should also notice that the ball is spinning.

You can try it with a bigger ball, but it's hard work. Such hard work that you might need to sit down and maybe have a snooze to recover.

Don't worry! You can use a hairdryer.

3. Angle the hairdryer at about 45 degrees, switch it on (preferably on a cool setting) and let go of the ball. All you have to do now is marvel at how the ball hovers in the air.

What's happening?

It's all down to a thing called the Bernoulli effect. The airstream flowing round the ball travels faster than the surrounding air. This means there is less pressure inside the airstream so the ball stays inside it. The lower pressure causes enough lift to balance out gravity and

keep the ball in the air. Lift is really important because it's what makes planes fly.

It's called the Bernoulli effect after Dutch–Swiss mathematician Daniel Bernoulli. We came up with our own effect. The Punk-Science effect. It requires a much bigger ball. Which reminds me . . . Here's our much bigger ball . . . But it won't work and you'll end up looking as stupid as Brad does.

FACT

At the moment spaceships are fuelled by chemicals like hydrogen, kerosene or hydrazine. These are OK, but the fuel runs out a bit too quickly if you want to go on a long journey. The future of space travel might be with sails. Not like on a sailing ship, but a big solar sail on a space-ship that uses the push of the sunlight to make it go.

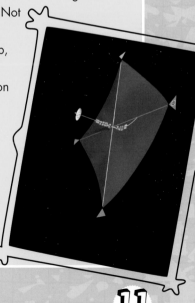

Fizz Bang Rockets

Space travel relies on rockets, and many space agencies develop their own type of rocket, but they all use the same principles. You can be a part of the Space Academy Punk Science, or SAPS for short.

Here's how to make your own rocket.

You'll need:
- Water
- A film canister
- A fizzy tablet for upset stomachs

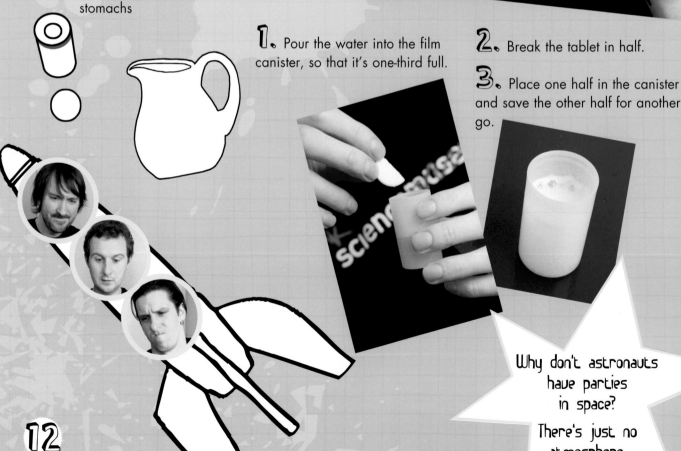

1. Pour the water into the film canister, so that it's one-third full.

2. Break the tablet in half.

3. Place one half in the canister and save the other half for another go.

Why don't astronauts have parties in space?

There's just no atmosphere.

4. This is where you'll have to kick it up a gear and move fast. Place the lid on the canister, making sure it's on good and tight. Now give it a good shake.

5. Place the canister lid-side down and get out of the way. You can cower under a table if you like – it won't help, but you can if you want to.

This has a messy rating of 5 out of 5. Do it in the garden if possible. If you are launching it inside, place the rocket on a tray. Otherwise you might ruin the carpet.

RATINGS

Difficulty
✈ ✈ ✈ ✈ ✈

All that dropping, shaking and hiding – you're going to need good coordination.

Messy
✈ ✈ ✈ ✈ ✈

This will splat all over the floor . . . urgghh!

Grown-up helper
✈ ✈ ✈ ✈ ✈

Only to help tidy up afterwards.

Time ⏱

This should take you about **10 minutes**.

ready . . .

Blast off!

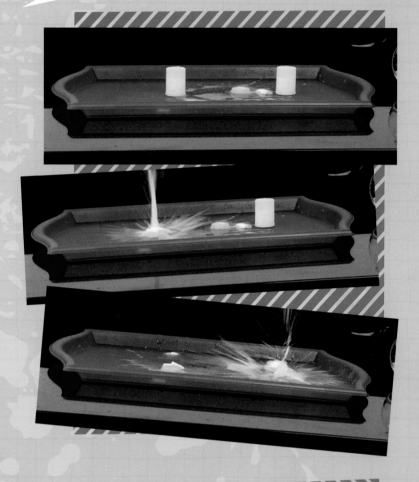

What's happening?

We like rocket science to be easy. Here is some easy rocket science, thanks to Sir Isaac Newton and his Third Law of Motion, which states that 'for every action there is an equal and opposite reaction'. In our rockets the force of the pop pushes the lid and contents out of the canister. That's the action. The **re**action is when the rocket goes in the opposite direction, up into the air. It's like swimming. When you do breaststroke you push the water back, but what happens? You move forward. The same thing happens with the rocket.

Inside the rocket little bubbles of carbon dioxide are fizzing. Eventually there's so much of it in the canister it starts squashing the water. But there's only so much squashing the water can take until it finally says, 'That's it! I'm leaving,' and with a big build-up of pressure the lid pops off, and the canister flies off into space or, failing that, a couple of metres in the air. If you do want to get into space, you need a pretty big rocket, with some pretty big fuel tanks. But that's just to get out of the Earth's atmosphere. If we launched rockets from the moon, we wouldn't need so much power or fuel because the force of gravity is much less there (you still need to get to the moon in the first place though!).

The BIG Idea

In the 1890s a very clever German chap named Otto Lilienthal thought he could use birds as the inspiration for a glider. We say he was clever, but once he'd designed these gliders he'd do something not very clever at all. He'd strap them on to himself and jump off cliffs and hills. Fortunately, a lot of the time it worked and he made some quite long and fairly well-controlled flights. He did this over two thousand times and put together some really good research as a result. It was so good the Wright brothers used his calculations to help them design their plane. Unfortunately for Otto, one time it didn't work and he died. But if it weren't for clever, courageous people doing things that are bit odd and not altogether sensible, then we might never have got off the ground. Remember, jumping off cliffs is bad for your health, even if it is in the name of science.

FACT

In 1919 John Alcock and Arthur Whitten Brown thought it would be a good idea to fly non-stop over the Atlantic in an open-topped biplane. Not as mad as it sounds though, because they made it and they were the first people to do it. However, they did crash-land in a bog, but that doesn't matter. Well done, chaps!

2004
Space Ship One is the first private craft to carry humans to the edge of space

Present day
Birds still fail to launch a successful space programme

2012
Predicted date for the first holidays in space on Space Ship One

2000
First crew arrive on the International Space Station. It's been continuously inhabited ever since

Timeline

1981
First Space Shuttle mission

1971
Concorde, the first supersonic passenger-carrying jet, crosses the Atlantic

1957
Russians put the first animal in space, a dog called Laika

1969
USA astronauts Neil Armstrong and Buzz Aldrin land on the moon

1961
Russians put the first human in space; he was called Yuri Gagarin

1938
Hannah Reitsch flies an early helicopter indoors at a sports stadium in Berlin

100 BC
Birds doing all the flying

AD 100
Yup, still mostly birds doing the flying

1010
A monk with wings attached jumps off Malmesbury Abbey. He flies a very short distance before breaking his legs

1488–1514
Leonardo Da Vinci designs a helicopter. It's never made. So birds are still in charge of the skies

1300s
Kites are used to carry people in China

Start here

1896
Otto Lilienthal dies in a glider accident after more than 2,000 flights. (See The Big Idea p. 15)

1783
Montgolfier Brothers challenge the birds by flying in a balloon

1903
Wright brothers make the first controlled powered flight

1852
First steam-powered airship is flown by Henri Giffard

1909
Louis Bleriot flies across the English Channel

1919
Alcock and Brown fly across the Atlantic (See Fact p. 15)

How do you grow a power station? Plant a lightbulb.

Energy

We're a bit suspicious of energy at Punk Science. Go on – ask why. Because it's sneaky. Come on – ask why it's sneaky. Because it can change its form many times, but it cannot be created or destroyed. Surely it can't just be us who think that's a bit peculiar! It would make the ultimate monster though, changing its form all the time, and no matter how hard people tried, there is no way of destroying it. Unfortunately, making a monster out of energy has proven quite difficult for our simple Punk Science brains. So, instead, to scare people we took photos of us first thing in the morning when we're getting out of bed. Which is one of the scariest sights in the world. Except for your parents dancing – now that is scary.

But we are not talking about scary things, we're talking about energy. Energy is a bit like a rubbish footballer, because it's always getting transferred. Energy is used in many different ways, and we can experience it in many different ways, for example as heat, or as light. When we use energy it doesn't just disappear, instead it is transferred into a different form.

Light and heat energy from the sun is taken in by plants and is transferred into chemical energy within the plant. The plant gets picked and we eat it, so the chemical energy inside the plant is transferred into chemical energy inside us. We then use that energy to help us do everything from walking to talking to breathing. The very same energy that we started with is again transferred through all that walking and talking into different forms like movement energy, heat energy and sound energy, and that energy will keep on going and going, transferring from one form to another and never being used up.

FACT

Our main source of energy, the sun, will stop burning. But, do not be afraid, it will not happen for a few billion years.

18

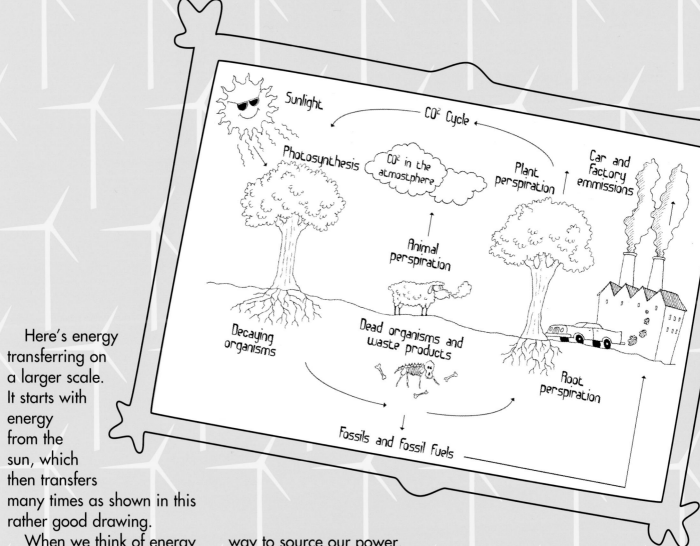

Sunlight

CO² Cycle

Photosynthesis

CO² in the atmostphere

Plant perspiration

Car and factory emmissions

Animal perspiration

Decaying organisms

Dead organisms and waste products

Root perspiration

Fossils and fossil fuels

Here's energy transferring on a larger scale. It starts with energy from the sun, which then transfers many times as shown in this rather good drawing.

When we think of energy we think of POWER. Power to destroy the world . . .

Oh, sorry, we, err, got a bit confused for a moment back there. It was all the talk of monsters earlier. Forget about the 'destroying the world' bit. Let's think about power. We can get power in lots of ways, and some big-brained people spend a lot of time trying to work out which is the best

way to source our power. We've got some examples of ways we harness energy, in the experiments you will try a bit later on. You can make your own tiny turbine which you can use to demonstrate wind power – not the farting sort! You can also use solar power to make a cooker, and hydro power, which is the power generated by water. What we don't

do an experiment for is perhaps our favourite form of generating power: biomass.

Biomass power comes from burning wood, food waste, and get this . . . poo. Yes, poo. We haven't made this up. In fact there are several power stations that burn poo in order to generate power. Which is not to be sniffed at, quite literally.

Rolling Tin

DO THIS AT TRY HOME!

For this experiment you will need to have a gravy container or something like it. Our advice is to ask for gravy on everything so it gets used up. We tried it and it worked: we had gravy on toast, gravy on ice cream, gravy on cornflakes and sometimes we had gravy on gravy. There is one very minor problem with this idea. It's disgusting! You could, however, use any sort of round and fat cardboard container.

Let's get started . . .

You'll need:
- A round cardboard container with a plastic lid at one end
- 3 screws
- A large elastic band
- Sticky tape
- Scissors

What's so good about stored energy?
It's got potential.

1. Playing with our cars is good, but it can be a bit boring because they don't come back. So we are going to make something that does.

20

2. Make a hole in the bottom of the container and in the lid. Push the elastic band through the hole in the container so that a little loop pokes through to the outside. Slip a screw through the loop so the band doesn't spring back into the container.

3. Use a little tape to attach a screw to the middle of the elastic band inside the tin and push the other end of the band out through the hole in the lid. Secure it with the final screw and put the lid on.

4. Push the tin and watch it roll back.

What's happening?

The energy from your pushing the tin is transferred into the elastic band by the rolling of the tin. When the tin stops, the elastic band releases that energy as movement energy and the tin rolls back in the opposite direction.

RATINGS

Difficulty
✋✋✋✋✋

Hard to attach the elastic band.

Messy
✋✋✋✋✋

Only if you forget to empty the container first.

Grown-up helper
✋✋✋✋✋

Might need them to make the holes for you.

Time ⏱

This should take you about **10 minutes**.

FACT

Energy is measured in Joules. This is named after English physicist James Prescott Joule who, during middle of the nineteenth century, worked on the nature of heat and its relation to energy.

Tiny Turbine

We've got plenty of wind at Punk Science HQ, so it seems only right for us to make something wind powered. However, our wind is the smelly kind. It's probably for the best if you head outside to use your turbine. Or you could come and find us to power it, but do bring a gas mask.

DO THIS OUTSIDE!

Let's get started . . .

You'll need:

- A square piece of thin card
- Scissors
- A drawing pin
- A dowel rod (from craft shops or DIY stores)

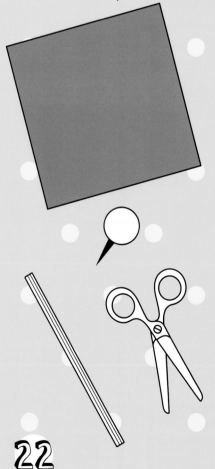

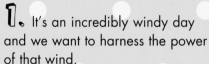

1. It's an incredibly windy day and we want to harness the power of that wind.

2. Cut towards the middle of the card from each corner.

Why is wind power so popular?

It has lots of fans.

22

3. Fold in a corner from each of your four sections.

4. Pin the folded card to the dowel rod.

5. The power of the wind will blow the tiny turbine around.

RATINGS

Difficulty

The pinning can be a bit tricky.

Messy

No mess, just wind.

Grown-up helper

Get your grown-up to put your pin in for you and do the cutting.

Time 🕐

This should take you about **10 minutes**.

What's happening?

We're using the power of the wind to turn our tiny turbine. This is similar to how large wind turbines work. The wind turns them and we use that to generate electricity. We'd need a lot of turbines to power the entire country though and it's only worth putting them in places where it's windy enough.

Solar-powered Oven

DO THIS AT TRY HOME!

If you like things powered by the sun and if you like your food too, you're in luck because this experiment combines them both. Don't expect a gourmet three-course meal though – not that you couldn't have a go at making one with your solar oven. It's just that we couldn't.

Let's have lunch

DO THIS OUTSIDE!

You'll need:

- A cardboard box like the sort delivery pizzas come in
- Kitchen foil
- A black bin liner
- A sliced tomato
- Cling film
- A sunny day!

RATINGS

Difficulty
✋✋✋✋✋
Does require a hot day to get it right.

Messy
✋✋✋✋✋
The tomato might be a bit messy

Grown-up helper
✋✋✋✋✋
Keep them away – they might want to eat the food.

Time 🕐
This should take you about **2 hours**.

1. We need our oven because we are starving.

2. Cover the cardboard box with foil.

24

3. Now stuff the box with the bin liner.

4. Wrap the slices of tomato in foil. Place the wrapped tomato in the box and cover the bottom part of the box with the cling film.

5. Leave your solar oven out in the sun for a couple of hours. Make sure the lid is angled to reflect the sun on to the food.

What's happening?

The foil reflects the heat from the sun down to where the food is. The black bin liner helps to retain the heat. The cling film seals warm air in to help heat up the box.

Solar power is more commonly used with photovoltaic cells to produce electricity. Photovoltaic cells work by converting sunlight into electricity – you may have seen them on roofs of some buildings. They can also be used to power calculators, watches and even cars.

6. When you return, your food should be ready to eat.

7. If you are not a complete greedy guts, you could even share.

25

Water Mill

DO THIS AT TRY HOME!

Water, water everywhere . . . oh no, we've left the taps running in the bathroom again. At least we think that's how the saying goes. There is lots of water around us so why not use it to generate power? This next experiment is a simple way of harnessing the power of water.

Why is hydropower relaxed?

Because it just goes with the flow.

Here's how to make your very own water mill.

You'll need:

- 6 yoghurt pots, empty of course
- 2 paper plates
- Sticky tape
- A dowel rod (from craft shops or DIY stores)
- A tap

FACT
There is enough energy in a bolt of lightning to toast 160,000 slices of bread.

1. Tape the yoghurt pots round one of the paper plates, open end to the outside.

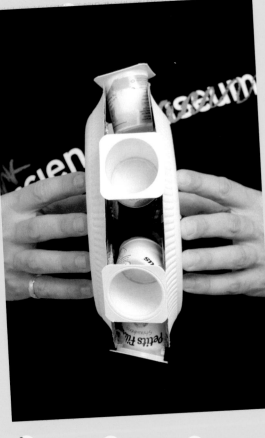

2. Now stick the other paper plate on the other side.

3. Put the rod through the middle of the plates. Try to make the holes a little larger than the rod so that it can spin freely.

4. Put your mill under the tap, turn the water on and watch it spin.

What's happening?

Water hits the yoghurt pots, which fill up and get heavier so they move downwards, making the wheel spin. Water has been used in this way to generate power since ancient times.

Hydropower can be used in several different ways, from harnessing the power of the tides to creating huge dams that concentrate the flow of water through turbines like the one we made – just a lot bigger.

RATINGS

Difficulty
✋ ✋ ✋ ✋ ✋

If we can make it, you can.

Messy
✋ ✋ ✋ ✋ ✋

You might get wet.

Grown-up helper
✋ ✋ ✋ ✋ ✋

Get them to make the holes in the plates, if you don't fancy.

Time ⏱
This should take you about **10 minutes**.

Two-ball Bounce

This is a good experiment to do after you've challenged a friend to bounce a tennis ball twice as high as it would normally bounce. Just wait to see their faces when you show them how to do it – you might even explain to them how it works as well.

Let's play ball.

You'll need:
- A tennis ball
- A football

1. We are bored of bouncing these balls because they don't go high enough.

2. Make the tennis ball bounce really high by dropping it on top of the football. Drop the balls at the same time.

3. See how far the tennis ball bounces. This time it goes incredibly high because it absorbs the energy of the football as well.

What's happening?
The football bounces and hits the tennis ball, giving it extra energy so it bounces higher than it normally would.

RATINGS

Difficulty
Dropping a ball on another ball – what could be easier?

Messy
When the ball bounces into things and breaks them.

Grown-up helper
Just make sure they're out of the way.

Time ⏱
This should take you about **2 minutes**.

28

The BIG Idea

The sun provides the majority of the energy for the Earth. Here are a few things you really should know about the sun: the sun is hot – that's pretty much it. No, there's more. The sun is really hot. Think of the hottest thing you can and times it by a million and you are beginning to get close to how hot the sun is. When we say close, obviously we don't mean get close to the sun – not that you could. But if you could . . . don't. Look, we are just trying to tell you that hot things are dangerous, so don't play with them. Not that you could, because it's the sun and its surface is about 6,000 degrees Celsius and its atmosphere is over two million degrees Celsius.

The sun is also very big; you could get about a million Planet Earths inside it. That is, if there weren't loads of nuclear reactions going on in the sun's core. It is these nuclear reactions that provide the sun's energy. There are nuclear reactions because the sun is huge and that means that there is a huge amount of gravity at its centre. So much gravity, in fact, that hydrogen atoms are squashed together so hard that they fuse. This fusion energy is what powers the sun, and therefore nearly everything on Earth. We say nearly everything because there are things that live around deep-sea vents that don't get any sunlight, let alone energy from it.

But nearly everything else gets its energy from the sun – things like humans and plants – and it is even in stuff that used to be alive. Like coal and gas, which are formed from animals and plants that died millions of years ago.

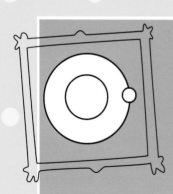

FACT

Hydrogen cells could be the future power for cars. Hydrogen is a more efficient fuel than petrol and will reduce urban pollution and could help prevent global warming.

What are the most powerful letters in the alphabet? N, R, G.

29

Also present day

We thought we should mention that, we didn't actually invent a perpetual-motion machine, because that would mean we'd be creating energy, which of course can't be done. We did make a nice cup of tea though, so it wasn't a complete loss in the Punk Science creativity department

Timeline

Present day

Punk Science invent the perpetual-motion machine – an ingenious device that gives out more energy than you put into it

1950

Rover make the world's first gas-turbine car, a car with a jet engine in it. Unfortunately it drinks a bit too much fuel so never goes into production

1884

Charles Parsons invents the steam turbine. Yes, more steam. But a steam turbine is better than a steam engine because it can be used to generate electricity more efficiently

1839

Edmund Becquerel discovers the photovoltaic effect. This is the way of getting electricity from light. It's what is used in solar panels

5 billion years ago
Sun forms. The source of all our energy and the most repeated thing in our timelines

65 million years ago
Dinosaurs die out and along with other animals and plant matter slowly become the fossil fuels we use today

start here

AD 1150
Tidal mills used in France and Britain to get energy

1712
Thomas Newcomen invents a steam engine that is used to pump water out of mines. This means more coal can be mined and paves the way for the use of fossil fuels

1829
A steam engine made by Robert Stephenson reaches the incredible speed of . . . wait for it . . . 29 miles per hour. What do you mean you're not impressed? Back then, that was faster than an elephant on roller skates going down a greasy hill. Come to think of it, it is still faster than an elephant on roller skates going down a greasy hill

1765
Watt makes his more efficient and a bit more famous steam engine

31

Electricity & Magnetism

This chapter is all about being attractive, if not a little shocking! So we thought we would test it out by dressing up as vampires, jumping out at some lovely ladies and shouting boo. We'd like to tell you it all went well and that we didn't get into any trouble at all, but the policeman says we are not allowed to.

This is all beside the point because we'd got it all wrong. The 'shocking and attractive' stuff was actually about electricity and magnetism, and if we'd only taken a second to look at the name of this chapter we would have avoided a lot of bother.

Electricity is handy – we use it to power pretty much everything, from TVs to toasters, and we can even use it to power our cars. Electricity doesn't always have to come from a plug socket; we can generate electricity in some really simple ways which we will show you in some of the experiments in this chapter.

Electricity is lazy. You might be thinking: Hang on, lightning is electricity but that doesn't look lazy. It looks quite the opposite – positively athletic in fact. We are sorry to break this news to you, but it *is* lazy, really lazy. Electricity always travels along the shortest path it can, so if there are two pathways for electricity to choose from, it will always take the one needing the least amount of effort.

Electricity likes passing through some things more than others. It finds it easy to go through metals, like iron and copper. Materials that allow electricity to flow through them are called conductors. This is nothing like the conductor of an orchestra, who if electricity was passed through them would probably get frizzy hair and very angry indeed. On the other hand, electricity doesn't like passing through materials like plastic and rubber. These types of materials are called insulators.

This chapter is not only about electricity, it is also

about magnetism. We all know magnets attract metals. Or do they? Magnets are actually a bit more picky than that – they only attract three metals, known as ferrous metals. These are iron, nickel and cobalt.

Non-ferrous metals like aluminium are not attracted to magnets, which is why when you place a magnet on most fizzy-drink cans it will not stick.

Magnets also have poles – not Polish people, or something you use to put up tents. Magnets have two poles, a north and a south, kind of like the Earth. They have to have both: you cannot have a south pole without a north – it just will not happen. This makes them sound like best buddies that cannot get enough of one another. North and south poles do attract each other, which is all very nice, but try pushing the same poles of two magnets together. Go on – try it. We dare you.

Did you actually try it or did you think you wouldn't bother because we would just tell you what happens anyway? Well, you were right. Like poles (which means two norths or two souths)

The BIG Idea

B | MICHAEL FARADAY, DISCOVERER of | D
ELECTRO MAGNETISM

Just because we use electricity to power modern devices and gadgets, it doesn't mean electricity itself is a modern thing – far from it. Ancient Greeks created static electricity by rubbing amber against a piece of fur. It did take quite a while longer for electricity to become useful.

One scientist who helped with this was Michael Faraday (top left). Born in London in 1791, Faraday did not have much of an education when it came to schools or universities; instead he learned through experimentation and some guidance from another scientist

called Humphrey Davy (top right). Faraday was a chemist as well as a physicist, but we are not interested in that at the moment. We want to look at how he realized that electricity and magnetism are forms of the same thing, something he unimaginatively called . . . electromagnetism. OK, it wasn't an achievement on the naming front, but it did lead to the first electric motor. Electric motors are turning millions of electrical machines around the world at this very moment.

repel. It doesn't matter how hard you push them together,

you will never get them to stay.

Bendy Water

Water can be troublesome. It can be too cold, or too hot, but temperature isn't important here, because with this experiment we're going to control the movement of water using an electrical field. Hope you don't mind getting on with it while we dry ourselves off.

Let's bend water.

You'll need:
- A tap
- A balloon
- Something woolly

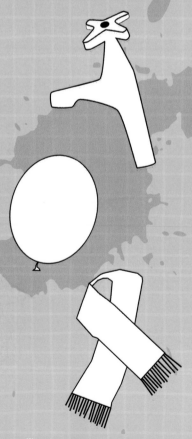

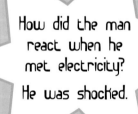

How did the man react when he met electricity?

He was shocked.

1. Challenge your friends to see who can make water bend without touching it. Using the power of the mind doesn't seem to work.

2. Using a karate chop means touching the water, which sort of defeats the object.

RATINGS

Difficulty
⚙ ⚙ ⚙ ⚙ ⚙
You have to get the charge up so it'll work.

Messy
⚙ ⚙ ⚙ ⚙ ⚙
You could get a bit wet.

Grown-up helper
⚙ ⚙ ⚙ ⚙ ⚙
Only to watch in awe.

Time 🕐
This should take you about **10 minutes**.

3. Here's how it should be done: blow up a balloon.

4. Rub the balloon against the woolly thing to build up a static charge.

5. Hold the balloon close to the flowing water and watch it bend.

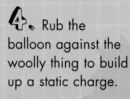

What's happening?

Everything is made up of atoms. Atoms themselves are made of even smaller things called protons, neutrons and electrons. When we create static electricity, we are making the electrons move from one atom to another. This means the atoms now have either extra electrons (which means it has a negative charge) or fewer electrons (which gives it a positive charge).

At first our balloon has positive and negative electrical charges in equal amounts. When it is rubbed against a material like wool, silk or cotton, this causes electrons to move on to the balloon from the material, giving the balloon a negative charge. The balloon then attracts the positive charges in the water because opposites attract, causing the water to bend its flow towards the balloon.

35

Electromagnet

When is a magnet not a magnet? When it's an electromagnet. It's only a magnet when you switch on the electric current. Switch off the electric current and it won't work any more. It's what they use to pick cars up with when they crush them. We thought the Punk Science car had been crushed once, but it turned out we'd just eaten way too much ice cream and couldn't fit in it any more. See what the heaviest thing is that you can pick up with your electromagnet. Remember not to switch it off while you're picking it up, otherwise it'll be sore feet all round.

GROWN-UP HELPER NEEDED!

Stick with us . . .

You'll need:

- Paper clips
- A screwdriver (a stainless-steel screwdriver might not work)
- One length of insulated wire from an electronics shop or DIY store
- A battery (size D)
- Sticky tape

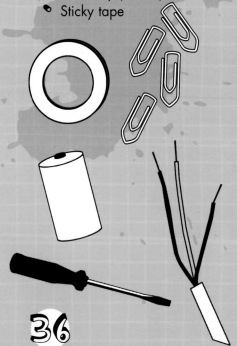

1. Trying to pick up paper clips with a screwdriver is a bit of a waste of time, not to mention silly. Unless, of course, you make the screwdriver into an electromagnet.

2. Tightly wrap the wire around the screwdriver a few dozen times. Make sure you use insulated wire, otherwise the electricity will short-circuit through the screwdriver shaft and the battery will overheat. Make sure you leave enough wire at each end to attach to the battery.

3. Attach one end of the wire to the bottom of the battery and the other end of the wire to the top. Use some tape to stick them down. Take care when connecting the wire ends to the battery because the wire can get a bit hot.

4. Now that you've got an electromagnet, picking up the paper clips is easy. If you want to drop them again, just disconnect the battery. Keep the battery connected for only a few seconds at a time. Your battery won't last long since the electromagnet draws a lot of electric current.

What's happening?

The screwdriver isn't a magnet, so how does this work? It is the electricity passing through the tightly coiled wire that makes a magnetic field so we can pick up the paper clips. Cut the electricity and the magnetism stops too.

FACT

Trains can run on magnets at very high speeds because they use electromagnets that switch on and off, propelling the train forward. They're called magnetic levitation or Maglev trains. They sound great, but there is one slight problem with them: the track costs millions of pounds so they're incredibly expensive – but who cares because they are pant-wettingly quick! A Japanese version of a Maglev train broke the world record travelling at an 'Ooh that's a bit quick' 361 miles per hour. Before you say, That's all well and good but I haven't been on one, we'd suggest taking a trip to China where they have a passenger Maglev train line up and running. Or you could just wait until the rest of the world catches up, which won't be easy, considering they are really fast trains.

RATINGS

Difficulty
⚙ ⚙ ⚙ ⚙ ⚙
It requires a bit of construction work.

Messy
⚙ ⚙ ⚙ ⚙ ⚙
The only messy things are the paper clips, and you pick them up.

Grown-up helper
⚙ ⚙ ⚙ ⚙ ⚙
They might need to check the wire doesn't get too hot.

Time 🕐
This should take you about **10 minutes**.

Make a Compass

We Punk Scientists are an intrepid bunch. We often go on long explorations – sometimes we'll leave the museum and be gone for up to, but not exceeding, 5 or even 10 minutes. It is impressive, but not always wise. Outside the museum is a bewildering place – there are pavements and post boxes and stuff. It can get really confusing.

FACT

All computers contain magnets and so does a lot of electrical equipment – tons of things, in fact, like vacuum cleaners, hairdryers, DVD players and cars.

Let's get started . . . .

You'll need:
- A needle
- A magnet
- A bowl of water
- A plastic bottle top

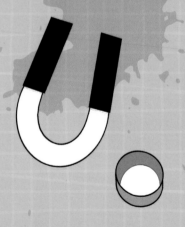

1. Oh dear, I think we might be lost.

2. No need to worry. We can construct a simple compass. Rub the needle with the magnet 50 times in the direction of the sharp end. Don't do it back and forth or it will not work.

Why are batteries so poor?

Because they're always being charged.

3. Place your bottle top in the bowl of water so that it floats. Now place the magnetized needle on top of the bottle top. You should see it spin round a little bit in the water and then stop.

4. One end will now point north and the other south. The trick is to know which is which, but at least now you're not heading east or west and have a 50:50 chance of going in the right direction. However, it does mean we're still half lost.

What's happening?

Our metal needle is made up of things called domains that are pointing in all different directions. You are trying to get all the domains that are in the metal to point in the same direction.

When you start they are pointing all over the place; using the magnet you make them point the same way, which is what makes the needle magnetic.

One end of the needle is then attracted to the pull of the earth's magnetic south pole and the other end to the magnetic north pole (see Fact p. 43).

RATINGS

Difficulty

⚙ ⚙ ⚙ ⚙ ⚙

It can be tricky to just stroke the needle one way.

Messy

⚙ ⚙ ⚙ ⚙ ⚙

This isn't messy.

Grown-up helper

⚙ ⚙ ⚙ ⚙ ⚙

To find you if you get lost.

Time 🕐

This should take you about **10 minutes**.

Lemon Battery

If you suck on a lemon, it won't make your face light up – it'll do quite the opposite. But a lemon can make a little light bulb light up. This experiment shows how to harness the power of the lemon by sticking stuff in it. No wonder they're so bitter.

Here's how to make a lemon battery.

You'll need:

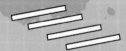

- 4 lemons
- 4 zinc strips
- 4 copper strips
- 5 wires with crocodile clips already attached
- An LED

(All of these things are available at high street electrical retailers . . . except the lemons).

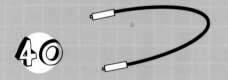

1. Push a zinc strip and a copper strip into each lemon.

2. Connect up the strips by fastening one clip to a zinc strip and the other to a copper strip on a different lemon; otherwise you are doomed to failure. Now you have to make a circuit.

Leave one connection from a copper strip free and another connection from a zinc strip free. These will be attached to the LED.

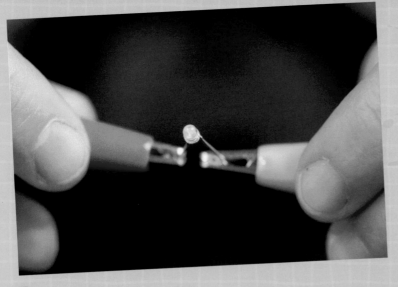

RATINGS

Difficulty
You need to get this exactly right and you'll still only get a faint light.

Messy
Maybe a bit of lemon-juice spillage.

Grown-up helper
To observe the wonder of lemons.

Time
This should take you about **10 minutes**.

3. Attach the two remaining clips to the LED to complete the circuit and watch it light up. If you darken the room, you'll be able to make out a faint light. Don't get too excited though, because you'd need hundreds of thousands of lemons to power your home so unless you've got an enormous lemon grove in your garden I'd stick to the electricity provided for you. You know, the stuff that comes from the plug socket.

4. Unless of course you can get hold of a massive lemon, like this.

What's happening?

Our copper and zinc strips are called electrodes. When we push them into the lemons, the acidic juice of the lemons acts as an electrolyte. An electrolyte is something that allows electricity to pass through it. This allows electrons to collect at one electrode, while the other electrode loses some of its electrons. It's this process that creates the electricity that powers our light.

Why is electricity intelligent?

Because it knows Watt is Watt.

Tiny Lightning

We mentioned before that lightning is lazy, but we're going to make lightning that is also very small. In fact, so incredibly minuscule it is almost the size of a Punk Scientist's brain. Now that is small. At least it might be . . . we not sure . . . we not think too good.

It's striking.

You'll need:

- A polystyrene sheet (from DIY stores)
- Something made of wool
- A darkened room
- A metal container
- A key

1. Rub the piece of polystyrene against your woolly thing.

Why did the piece of metal marry the magnet?

Because they were attracted to each other.

2. Make sure you're in a dark room.

RATINGS

Difficulty
⚙ ⚙ ⚙ ⚙ ⚙
A steady hand is needed to get this right.

Messy
⚙ ⚙ ⚙ ⚙ ⚙
Hard but not messy.

Grown-up helper
⚙ ⚙ ⚙ ⚙ ⚙
Get them to build up the charge. It can be hard work.

Time 🕐
This should take you about **10 minutes**.

3. Drop the metal container on the foam tile and with an incredibly steady hand put the key close to the container. Look out for the tiny spark from the container to the key.

4. Remember, micro-lightning is tiny so it's safe. Real lightning carries thousands of volts and is *really dangerous* so don't try playing with it or you'll end up looking like Brad.

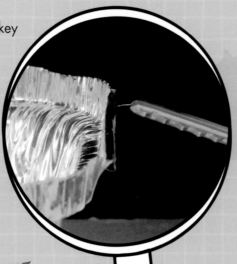

What's happening?

Like when we bent the water, we're using static electricity. We built up a charge on the foam, which then passes through the metal container and leaps to our key. Lightning is a much bigger version of this. The static charge leaps from clouds to the Earth.

FACT

The Earth has its very own magnetic field. This is what attracts a compass needle to point north. It's a weird thing the magnetic field – it's always on the move. We always think that magnetic north is at the North Pole, but it's not – it's currently somewhere in northern Canada, whereas the magnetic southern pole is just outside the Antarctic Circle off Wilkes Land. But it gets weirder because the North and South Poles can actually swap, and did swap 780,000 years ago.

1891
London gets electric street lighting – very handy, especially with all those cars that would be driving on the streets in a few years' time

How many Punk Scientists does it take to change a light bulb?

Three, one to hold the light bulb while the other two twist the ceiling round.

Timeline

1881
Lord Kelvin converts his house in Glasgow to be the first in Europe to have electric lights

1800
Alessandro Volta invents the first battery gets and so he gets to name the volt

1752
Benjamin Franklin flies a kite. Not very exciting really. But it was in a lightning storm and he did have a key attached to the bottom of the string. This was to show that lightning was electrical

5 billion years ago

Sun forms. OK, we didn't really need this one in here, but we thought it's in most of the others so why not?

start here

Ancient Geeks

. . . ahem, we mean *Greeks* . . . observe the strange phenomenon of static electricity

The equally

ancient Chinese

use compass-like devices

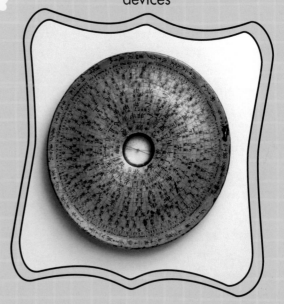

600 BC

Greeks describe magnetic qualities of lodestones

1646

Thomas Browne first uses the term 'electricity'

Forces

We're always pushing and pulling each other around. But we're not picking on each other – we're experimenting with forces. All forces are basically pushes or pulls.

So don't move a muscle, because we're surrounded by forces. Even standing completely motionless won't work because forces are still acting on us. Like the force of gravity. You probably already know a bit about gravity – it's the force that stops us from floating out into space, which is good, but it's also the force that makes your trousers fall down if you don't do them up properly, which is bad. **Gravity** is the force that gives us weight, because our weight is just a measurement of the effects of gravity on our bodies.

When an apple hit Sir Isaac Newton on the head, he thought, 'I'd better stop sitting around underneath dangerous fruit trees.' He also thought, 'Why do things fall down instead of up?' He went on to think that gravity was the force of attraction between two objects, and objects that have bigger mass (that's how much of something there is) will pull smaller objects towards them. The smaller objects will pull a bit themselves but not as much as the bigger object. That's a lot of thinking, which is what you need to do if you're going to write a mathematical theory explaining how gravity behaves. But don't start thinking that apple-based accidents stimulate the brain and make you a genius. We tried it on your behalf and pummelled our skulls with apples – it didn't make us more intelligent; in fact, it made us a bit queasy. Newton wasn't the first

46

person to think about gravity. The sixteenth-century Italian scientist Galileo performed a really simple experiment that you can try right now. Well, not right now . . . you'll need to read how to do it first.

Galileo used cannon balls for this, but we couldn't find any and even if we could we're all too weedy to pick them up. Take a big piece of paper and a tennis ball. Scrunch up the piece of paper so it's about the same size as the ball. Now hold them up and drop them. Despite the obvious weight difference they'll both hit the ground at almost the same time. This is because no matter how heavy something is, gravity pulls it down at the same speed.

Gravity pulls things, but what about a force that pushes things? How about upthrust? When you're in the water it pushes you up. If you're wondering why sometimes things sink, it's because those objects are too dense for upthrust to hold them up. Upthrust was first thought about by Archimedes, who was a great thinker from ancient Greece. Unfortunately he did it in rather embarrassing circumstances. He was in the bath and noticed when he got in that he pushed the water out of the way. The story says he got a bit excited and ran round the streets telling everyone and shouting, 'Eureka!' without putting any clothes on first. We don't care how important your discovery is, you've always got time to put your pants on before you start shouting in public.

Upthrust works like this: let's say we're on a boat – we'll call it the *Punktanic*, like the *Titanic*, that big ship that sank . . . maybe it's not such a good example, but as we can't be bothered to think of another it'll have to do. The *Punktanic* will float if it is lighter than the water it pushes out of the way. If the *Punktanic* gets heavier than the water it pushes out of the way, then it will sink. So, if we had two *Punktanic*s, one made of hollow plastic and the other made of stone, our light hollow plastic one is lighter than the water it pushes out of the way so it floats but our stone ship is heavier so it sinks. Luckily water is pretty heavy – have you ever tried to carry a full bucket? – so even big metal ships can float, as they weigh less than the water they push aside.

It's time to slow things down, and a force that is pretty good at that is friction. **Friction** happens when two surfaces rub together; the amount of friction will depend on how rough or smooth the surfaces are and how hard the two surfaces are pushed together. For example, if you rub your hands together, you'll experience friction. Your hands will also get hot because heat is produced as a result of friction. The more you push your hands together the more friction you get and the harder it will be to move them against each other.

squeeze!

Submarine

TRY THIS DO AT HOME!

Submarines are lucky – unlike ships they get to choose between floating and sinking or something in the middle, which we at Punk Science call flinking or soating (we're working on these words). This next experiment shows you how to flink or soat (sorry, we're still working on these words . . . it's hard thinking of new words! Maybe you should try to come up with something better).

Let's make a submarine.

You'll need:
- A 2-litre bottle
- Water
- A pen top
- Plasticine
- A paper clip

1. Another thing on Jon's list of things he wants to be is a diver. Let's leave him to think about that while you make a submarine using this stuff. Fill the bottle full of water – right to the top.

RATINGS

Difficulty
⚓ ⚓ ⚓ ⚓
Don't wobble the bottle once the submarine is in.

Messy
⚓ ⚓ ⚓ ⚓
It's not messy unless you spill the water.

Grown-up helper
⚓ ⚓ ⚓ ⚓
Only to watch the magic happen.

Time ⏰
This should take you about **10 minutes**.

Why do celebrities like gravity?

Because it helps them keep their feet on the ground.

2. If your pen top has a hole in the top, use a tiny bit of plasticine to block it up so that no air can escape. Don't plug the bottom as well or it won't work. Make a submarine shape out of the remaining plasticine and push the paper clip into it. Then hook the paper clip to the pen top.

3. Making sure that the pen top is full of air, place it in the bottle. Put the bottle top back on.

4. Make the submarine sink by squeezing the bottle. It will rise again when you let it go.

What's happening?
When we get the submarine to settle beneath the surface, it's called neutral buoyancy. Which just means it's neither floating nor sinking. When we squeeze the bottle, the air inside the pen lid gets squashed or compressed, allowing more water inside the pen lid so it sinks. When we stop squeezing the bottle, the air in the pen lid expands again, pushing the water out and making it light enough to float back up again.

Hard Liquid

Liquid can't be hard, can it? If it's custard it can be. Try this experiment and be as amazed as we were at just how odd custard is.

Let's rock.

You'll need:
- 200g custard powder
- A mixing bowl
- 100ml water
- A spoon
- A potato masher

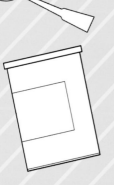

FACT
Mass is how much of something there is, whereas weight is dependent on how much gravity is acting on you.

1. Pour most of the custard powder into the bowl and add most of the water. Mix with the spoon. When adding your ingredients always use less at first – that way you can add some more if you need to. Remember, it's almost impossible to take stuff out once you've mixed it in. If you find your mixture is too watery, add more custard powder, and if you find it's too powdery, add more water. It should be a similar consistency to slightly soft ice cream.

2. Now gently rest the potato masher on the custard and watch it sink into the custard like it's quicksand.

3. Take the masher out and try hitting the custard with more force. It should bounce back.

4. When you are finished find a creative way to get rid of the custard.

What's happening?

Custard is a 'non-Newtonian' fluid, which means it doesn't act like a liquid should. When you apply small forces, it flows like a fluid. When you apply a bigger force, it thickens and acts more like a solid.

What force can you put on your dinner?

Gravy-ty.

RATINGS

Difficulty

⚓ ⚓ ⚓ ⚓

Pretty easy but you have to make quite thick custard.

Messy

⚓ ⚓ ⚓ ⚓

Custard splatting is messy.

Grown-up helper

⚓ ⚓ ⚓ ⚓

Only to help tidy up afterwards.

Time 🕐

This should take you about **10 minutes**.

51

Heavy Lifter

DO THIS AT TRY HOME!

Books are heavy, but that doesn't bother us because we can lift them with a straw. Don't believe us? Well, you're probably right not to. We don't look very strong, but we don't need to be when we've got the mighty power of science on our side.

Here's how to lift some books.

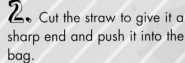

You'll need:
- A resealable freezer bag
- Sticky tape
- A straw
- Scissors
- Some heavy books

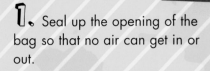

1. Seal up the opening of the bag so that no air can get in or out.

2. Cut the straw to give it a sharp end and push it into the bag.

What is the centre of gravity?

The letter V.

52

3. Now put the books on top of the bag.

4. Blow through the straw into the bag and the books will start to rise.

What's happening?

The air we blow in becomes compressed inside the bag. This raises the pressure of the air inside the bag, which pushes on the bag and in turn on the floor and the books, lifting the books. It's just like when you pump air into your bike tyres and they can take your weight.

RATINGS

Difficulty
⚓ ⚓ ⚓ ⚓

Don't pierce both sides of the bag.

Messy
⚓ ⚓ ⚓ ⚓

Only messy if you spit a lot when you blow.

Grown-up helper
⚓ ⚓ ⚓ ⚓

Get them to cut the straw – saves you the bother.

Time 🕐
This should take you about **5 minutes**.

FACT

Gravity pulls us down with less force on the moon (above left) because it is smaller and has the same density as the Earth – so you weigh a sixth of what you would weigh on Earth (below left).

On other planets the effect of gravity is also different: on Jupiter (right) you would weigh more than twice what you do on Earth whereas on Mars (below right) you'd weigh less than half. But the big one is the sun, where you'd be 270 times heavier than on Earth, you big lardy.

Egg Trick

This is not so much an experiment as an eggs-periment . . . sorry about that. This is an opportunity to test out some forces and your kung-fu skills too. It's really important to practise before you impress your friends with this. This experiment has the potential to be really messy and you don't want to be scrubbing the carpet when you should be doing more experiments.

RATINGS

Difficulty
⚓ ⚓ ⚓ ⚓
Practise without the eggs first.

Messy
⚓ ⚓ ⚓ ⚓
Get it wrong and you'll get egg on your face – and on the floor for that matter.

Grown-up helper
⚓ ⚓ ⚓ ⚓
To make sure you don't break their glasses.

Time 🕐
This should take you about **10 minutes**.

HI-YAAAA!!

You'll need:
- 4 glasses
- A place mat
- Water
- 4 slim cardboard tubes
- 4 raw eggs

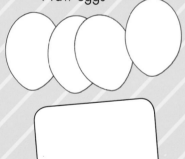

1. Half-fill the glasses with water and put the place mat on them slick side down. Have one end of the mat sticking out further than the other. This will make it easier to hit.

2. Place the tubes above each glass. Now put the eggs on top of them.

3. Using all your skill, hit the place mat out with one sharp blow. You'll need to hit with the palm of your hand and to the side of the mat so it slides out the opposite end. We'd recommend doing this outside – it could be messy.

54

4. The eggs land in the glasses unbroken. Ah yeah!

What's happening?

There are a few forces at work here. There is a little friction when the mat is hit away. However, it's a lack of force acting on the eggs that means they don't fly off with the mat. Then gravity pulls the eggs down and it's upthrust that keeps the eggs floating in the glasses.

DO THIS OUTSIDE!

massive object (sun)

fabric is warped by massive object ↓

fabric of space-time

planets in orbit

The BIG Idea

Albert Einstein is probably the most famous scientist ever; well, he is at Punk Science HQ anyway. We thought it was because he looked a bit mad. It turns out it was actually because he came up with several groundbreaking theories – and he looked a bit mad. One of his theories had to do with gravity. It was called the General Theory of Relativity. Yeah OK, we didn't know what any of that means either. But after we read up about it, we discovered it was about gravity.

We know that gravity is what keeps our feet on the ground, but it also does a lot more things and one of those things is that it keeps the Earth in orbit around the sun. Newton wrote all about how gravity behaves; Albert Einstein realized how gravity bends space. It sounds pretty difficult to understand and it is. We were scratching our heads about it for weeks, until we realized it wasn't the thinking making us scratch our heads – we all actually had a bad case of nits.

Think of all of space like your bed. If you put an object like a football or a rucksack filled with books, on top of your bed they will cause dips in the sheet; the heavier the object, the bigger the dip. Those dips pull stuff that's nearby into them. Roll some smaller objects like tennis balls across the bed and you'll see them pulled in by the heavier objects.

Now think of your objects as planets and the bedsheet as the fabric of space – time and that is pretty much how gravity works. We might know how it works, but we're not completely certain why things are attracted to each other. Whoever does come up with the answer will go down in history. Go on then, start working on it.

55

1919
Einstein publishes his general Theory of Relativity, showing that gravity is formed by the warping of the fabric of space – time

Timeline

Isaacus Newton Eq Aur.

The Hon.ble Robert Boyle.

1659
Robert Boyle shows that objects in a vacuum fall at the same rate

1687
Newton publishes his Three Laws of Motion.

Beginning of the universe

13.7 billion years ago, give or take a few million years. These forces have been around a long time – they got going as the universe started to form

start here

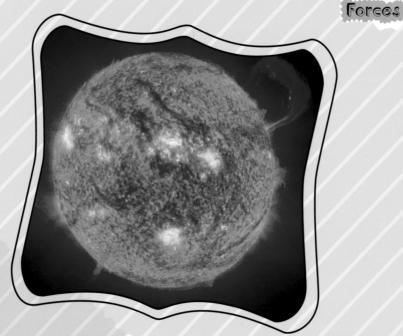

5 billion years ago

Sun forms. The gravity from the sun is what keeps the Earth in orbit. This is pretty old stuff – almost as old as Brad, and he's ancient

Early seventeenth century

Galileo conducts experiments – some real and some just inside his mind – to show how forces work

Third century BC

Archimedes paves the way in explaining what forces do

57

Light & Sound

Sound is seriously speedy stuff, but light is so fast it makes sound look like a sack of potatoes stuck in quick-drying cement. That's because light is the fastest thing in the universe: it travels at 186,000 miles per second – now that is fast.

We like fast things! The faster the better. We feel the need, the need for speed. For example, we like fighter jets that can go faster than the speed of sound. 'What's the speed of sound?' we hear you cry. Go on, say, 'What's the speed of sound?' Come on, say it out loud! We don't care if it makes you look like a freak. Thank you, now that wasn't so hard, was it? The

speed of sound at sea level in normal conditions is about 761 miles an hour.

. . . Actually, we had a chat about that, and that's a bit fast for our liking.

We want something that's still fast but a bit slower than the speed of sound. That's why we prefer racing cars speeding round a track, making lots of tremendously loud noises. No, on reflection that would probably make us feel queasy. We need something that's fast but not as fast as racing cars. Maybe something like riding your bike down a really steep hill. Oooh, yeah! Hang on a moment, we're still a bit concerned that could be a bit racy too – we might

accidentally swallow bugs. We could run as fast as we could, but that would be hard work, so let's forget that.

It's settled, Punk Scientists like fast things, but the fastest thing we would actually do is get up from a chair really quickly. And that's only if there are cushions on the floor, just in case we get a rush of blood to our heads and fall over. Just to make it absolutely clear, there is no way we'd ever want to travel at the speed of sound, let alone the speed of light.

There are more things to light than its speed. The main source of light on Earth is the sun. The sun throws light out in all directions and some of it reaches the Earth. Even

though light is fast, it still takes it around eight minutes to get from the sun to the Earth.

We think of light as colourless, but the mighty Sir Isaac Newton showed us that light is actually made up of lots of different colours. He did this by passing light through a prism (see above), which breaks the light up so we can see it is actually a mixture of colours. More of that in our colour-wheel experiment (see p. 64).

We can't see in the dark because we need light to see. When we look at something, only light of certain colours is bouncing off it and into our eyes – that's how we see things. So, if a ball looks red, it is because the ball is absorbing all the other wavelengths of light but letting the red wavelengths bounce back to your eye.

With sound it's about vibrations. Sound can only work if it's got something to vibrate. Usually it vibrates air, but sound can pass through water and solid objects too. When sound passes through air, it makes the air vibrate. Air is made up of things

The BIG Idea

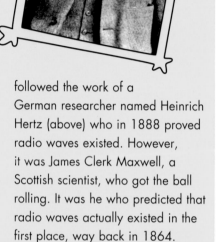

Radio waves are incredible things – they can carry information that we can listen to and see. But get this: we can't actually see or hear the radio waves themselves, we can only hear the information they carry, and that's just weird. But radio waves are like the light waves we told you about earlier; they are part of the same family of electromagnetic waves. The music we hear is actually smaller radio waves that travel on a larger carrier radio wave. This method is also used for some TVs to get their pictures and sounds, and it's what our mobile phones use so we can text and chat to each other.

We're also looking for aliens by using telescopes that listen out for any radio signals that they might be sending out. These enormous dishes are pointed out into space in the hope that an alien might send us a message, hopefully a nice one.

An Italian engineer called Guglielmo Marconi (right) was the first person to develop a practical and commercial system to send radio signals in 1895. He

followed the work of a German researcher named Heinrich Hertz (above) who in 1888 proved radio waves existed. However, it was James Clerk Maxwell, a Scottish scientist, who got the ball rolling. It was he who predicted that radio waves actually existed in the first place, way back in 1864.

We've moved on a bit from the radio signals that were sent back then. Now we're using digital radio signals. With digital radio, more information is sent than with normal radio signals.

called molecules. When molecules are vibrated or knocked they bang into other air molecules and pass the sound along. It's like the air is playing pass the parcel,

but with noises instead of presents. You can see how sound works in our string mobile phone experiment (see p. 68).

59

Why Is the Sky Blue and the Sun Yellow?

This experiment is proof that Punk Scientists don't shy away from the big questions. We tried to, but someone said they'd flick our ears if we didn't do an experiment to explain why the sky was blue and the sun yellow. To do this experiment you need to take a moment to think.

Let's make a science rainbow . . .

You'll need:
- A clear plastic container
- Water
- Milk
- A spoon
- A darkened room
- A torch
- A scary Brad is optional

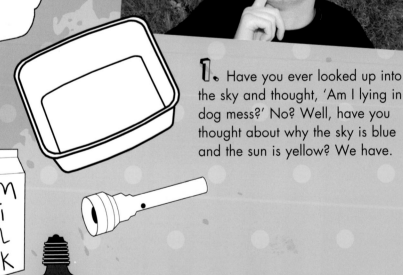

1. Have you ever looked up into the sky and thought, 'Am I lying in dog mess?' No? Well, have you thought about why the sky is blue and the sun is yellow? We have.

RATINGS

Difficulty
Too little milk and it won't work.

Messy
Only if you spill the milk, but don't cry over it.

Grown-up helper
Get them to hold the torch.

Time
This should take you about **10 minutes.**

2. Fill the container with water and add a few tablespoons of milk. Mix it a bit.

3. In a darkened room put the torch against the end of the container and switch it on. Look at the container. It will appear blue close to the torch end.

Which day of the week has the most light?
Sunday.

4. Look at the opposite end and you'll see it appears yellow.

What's happening?

This is what happens in the sky. In the same way the light bounces off the milk particles, light passing through the sky bounces off particles. The blue light gets bounced around the most, so whatever direction you look at you see a blue colour. However, when we look down the end of the container we see yellow. This is because when the light has further to travel and has more particles to pass through, it is only the red and yellowy light that makes it all the way. So we have yellow and red sunsets and sunrises because the sun is low in the sky and the light coming from it has to pass through more of the atmosphere.

61

Evil-ghost Toy

This experiment is something they used to do in theatres to frighten the audience. We'll show you how to do it so you can frighten your friends and family. But first there are a few things you need to know.

Let's get started . . .

You'll need:

- A toy
- A piece of cardboard
- A sheet of perspex from a DIY store
- A darkened room
- A torch

1. Ghosts are extremely scary. However, as ghosts probably don't exist you'll need science to create the illusion of one.

2. Place the toy as shown in the diagram below.

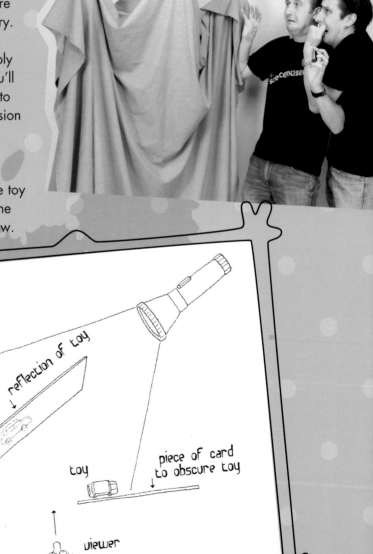

reflection of toy

perspex

toy

piece of card to obscure toy

viewer

Why is the dark stupid?

Because it's dim.

3. The room needs to be quite dark for this to work. Shine the torch along the angled piece of perspex.

4. Get someone to look and give them a good old-fashioned fright with your ghost toy.

What's happening?

The toy should appear in the perspex in a ghostly form. You are seeing the reflected light from the toy hitting the perspex and then bouncing back to where you are looking at it from.

Colour Wheel

Colour is controversial stuff. We know because we argued for ages about what colour the Punk Science uniforms should be. Brad wanted pink, Jon wanted puce and Dan wanted turquoise. In the end we had to go for black because that's all they had in the shop. You can try making a colour wheel using different colours to the ones we suggest and see what happens. It'll be rubbish, but try it anyway.

Colour me up, Punk.

You'll need:

- White cardboard
- A set of compasses
- A sharp pencil
- A ruler
- Coloured pens/pencils
- String

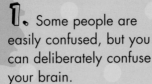

1. Some people are easily confused, but you can deliberately confuse your brain.

2. Draw a circle on the card using the compasses. Then divide the circle into seven sections. Colour in the sections like the diagram below. Make sure you use red, orange, yellow, green, blue, indigo and violet.

3. Make two holes and thread the string through. Join the two ends with a knot.

4. Wind up the string.

5. Pull the string at both ends. Watch the wheel spin and see the colours merge into one.

What's happening?

This happens because all the colours mixed together make white. When the circle spins, our brains do not work quickly enough to see each separate colour, so we see them at the same time, as white.

RATINGS

Difficulty
♡ ♡ ♡ ♡ ♡

Unless you use perfect colours, it won't come out white – probably just a greyish colour.

Messy
♡ ♡ ♡ ♡ ♡

You might get covered in pen.

Grown-up helper
♡ ♡ ♡ ♡ ♡

To make the holes.

Time 🕑
This should take you about **10 minutes**.

What colour is a burp? Burple.

Periscope

DO THIS AT TRY HOME!

Mirrors can be used in many different ways. One way we like to use mirrors is to check ourselves out to see how beautiful we are. It doesn't take us very long. Another use for mirrors is this next experiment.

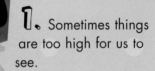

Let's make a periscope.

You'll need:

- 2 1-litre juice cartons
- Scissors
- 2 small mirrors, wider than the juice cartons

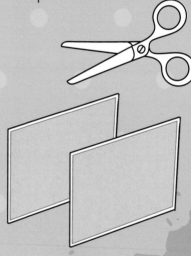

1. Sometimes things are too high for us to see.

2. Sometimes trying to climb up to see them ends in disaster.

3. Sometimes it's better to make a periscope. Cut the top off both cartons.

4. Cut a square hole at the bottom end of each carton.

5. Cut a slot in the side of each carton for the mirrors to go in at a 45-degree angle.

RATINGS

Difficulty
🎧🎧🎧🎧🎧
Get the angle right or you'll see nothing.

Messy
🎧🎧🎧🎧🎧
Only the rubbish from the cartons.

Grown-up helper
🎧🎧🎧🎧🎧
To help with the cutting.

Time 🕐
This should take you about **10 minutes**.

What do musical instruments surf on?

Sound waves.

6. Slot the cartons together with the holes on opposite sides and slide the mirrors in so that they face each other.

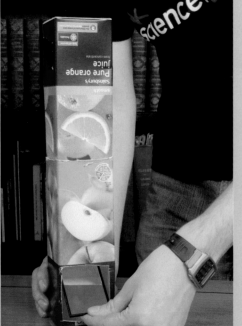

7. The periscope works. But sometimes what you see won't be particularly pleasant. Truly hideous.

What's happening?

It works by light hitting the first mirror and bouncing down from the first mirror to the second, and then bouncing to your eye. Periscopes were used on submarines to see what's happening on the surface from underwater (but modern subs use electronic sensors).

String Mobile Phone

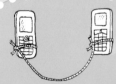

We're always calling each other – not with phones though because we haven't got any. Instead we just shout to each other, which can be embarrassing if you're trying to have a private conversation about whether or not you put clean pants on this morning, especially if you're on the bus or in the library. Rest assured, this next experiment is a cost-effective solution.

Let's get started.

You'll need:
- 2 paper or plastic cups
- Scissors
- A long piece of string

1. Mobile phones can be a bit expensive. But don't worry if you can't afford one – we've come up with a great alternative. It's really easy to make as well.

2. Make a small hole in the bottom of each cup.

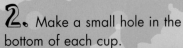

3. Take one end of the string and poke it through the bottom of the cup.

4. Tie a big knot inside the cup so the string doesn't fall out. Repeat this with the other end of the string and the other cup. Stretch the string so it's extremely tight; otherwise it won't work.

5. If you talk into one cup then the person at the other end of the string should be able to make out what you are saying. It doesn't sound like a real phone but it's much cheaper so who cares.

What's happening?

The line has to be tight because sound is passed down the string as vibrations. If the string is slack, the vibrations won't be carried and you won't hear anything.

RATINGS

Difficulty
Easy.

Messy
Not a bit.

Grown-up helper
With the scissors and the knots.

Time
This should take you about **5 minutes**.

FACT

Sound is measured in decibels, named after Alexander Graham Bell, the Scottish inventor who was first to develop a working telephone. You might have spotted that the word decibel and the name Alexander Graham Bell aren't that similar. This is because sound was originally measured by the bel, but it was too big. The unit we use is a tenth of this ('deci' means tenth) – that's how we get a decibel. Yeah, not so clever now, or maybe you are because you now know another fact.

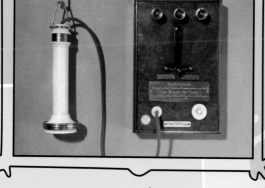

69

Timeline

1925
John Logie Baird invents the mechanical television. A box of light, but don't watch too much of it

1895
Wilhelm Rontgen discovers X-rays. We use these to look inside our bodies. We tried looking inside our bodies by staring into each other's mouths, but it didn't really work; the only thing we discovered is that Dan needs to brush his teeth

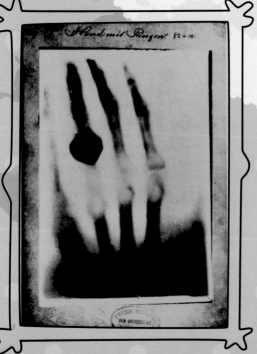

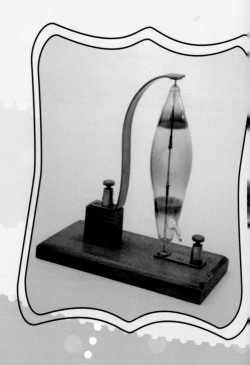

1878
Joseph Swan patents the lightbulb

70

5 billion years ago

Sun forms. Yes, we know you know this already. But without the sun there is no light so we need it again

start
here

1608

Galileo makes his telescope, which magnified an object three times. Imagine everything three times bigger – it would take you ages to eat your dinner

FACTS

❧ A quiet library will measure between 20 and 30 decibels.
❧ A normal talking level is about 50 decibels.
❧ The noise in your classroom will be on average between 60 and 80 decibels.
❧ A road drill is about 100 to 110 decibels.
❧ A jet taking off 25 metres away from you is 165 decibels.

FACT

Laser stands for Light Amplification by Stimulated Emission of Radiation. Lasers are a form of light that comes in a really narrow beam. We like them because they get used in space films, but they're used here on Earth in DVD players, measuring devices and in surgery to correct people's vision.

1842

Christian Doppler discovers that the pitch and frequency of a sound change depending on whether the sound is travelling towards or away from you. The Doppler effect is why the tone of a siren drops as it goes past your ears. Nee-nah-nee-nah-nee-noh-nee-noh . . .

Chemistry

Chemistry has a lot to do with getting a reaction. But we don't mean 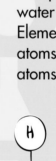 the sort of reaction you get by wearing your pants on your head and jumping up and down making monkey noises. Believe us, we tried it, but people just point at you and call you names like 'smelly pants head', which can be tiresome.

We mean a chemical reaction, where substances react with others to produce something different. It's like if you mixed us three Punk Scientists together you'd get something altogether new, like a big-nosed idiot with floppy ginger hair.

All reactions are either endothermic or exothermic. An exothermic reaction is one that produces heat and an endothermic reaction is one that consumes heat. We've got examples of these reactions in the experiments later on. Don't jump ahead though, because we've got some more stuff you need to know about chemistry first.

Everything we'll be experimenting with will be made up of elements, most probably in the form of a compound. Elements are things like hydrogen and oxygen. They are the basic building blocks of chemistry, which you use to make

H_2O

CO_2

other things like compounds. Compounds are things like water and carbon dioxide. Elements are made up of atoms, which are tiny, and atoms are made up of protons, neutrons and electrons, which are even tinier, and they're made up of even smaller things, which we won't go into because there are a few even smaller things after that and we could be here all day.

Elements are special because you can combine them with other elements to make a compound, but an element on its own cannot be broken down to make anything else. Think of elements as bricks. You can use lots of different bricks to make all sorts of buildings and these buildings are your compounds. But a brick on its own will only ever be a brick.

Let's forget about bricks. Obviously we don't mean forget what bricks are, otherwise you might use one as a football or try to eat one and that's less fun than wearing pants on your head, jumping up and down and making monkey noises. Try it – you'll see what we mean. But before you do, let's try some of the experiments.

The BIG Idea

One of the fathers of modern chemistry, Antoine Lavoisier was born in Paris in 1743. He was a very busy man because he wasn't just a chemist, but a tax collector, a geologist, an economist, a social reformer and a lawyer too. He concentrated on the chemistry though, and started out by making things explode better by improving gunpowder to make it smokeless and maybe most importantly to blow up more. Lavoisier then went on to show that water was made up of two elements, which he named oxygen and hydrogen. This was important stuff and led to Lavoisier coming up with theories about how and why things burned. It was quite a step forward.

Among his other achievements he also was the first to list the elements. The three of us at Punk Science were really impressed and were thinking he must have been rewarded for all this great work. Imagine our shock when we realized that he wasn't given loads of money or medals or even a box of chocolates. No, instead he was beheaded. Remember, science is important, but don't lose your head over it.

He wasn't beheaded for his scientific work – it was because of his involvement in the government, which didn't go down too well when the French Revolution happened. With this in mind, we're pretty glad we're Punk Scientists and not Punk Government Ministers, because we need our heads for stuff like wearing hats.

Fizz Fountain

DO THIS AT TRY HOME!

DO THIS OUTSIDE IF POSSIBLE!

We're going to make a fountain, but not a water fountain – a fizz fountain. This is going to get very messy, so this would be a good time to check the weather because you're going to need to go outside for this one. We'll give you a minute to have a look out of the window to see what it's like. Have you checked? If the weather's rubbish, save this experiment for another day and try the next one. If it's OK, then here's what you need.

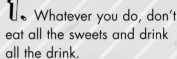

Let's start making it.

You'll need:

- A sheet of A4 card
- Sticky tape
- A toothpick
- Mints – hard outer, soft centre (some brands work better than others)
- Diet fizzy drink in a plastic bottle

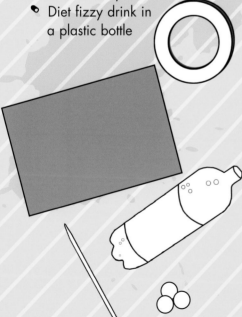

1. Whatever you do, don't eat all the sweets and drink all the drink.

2. In order to get as many sweets in the drink as we can (it works better with more sweets) we're going to make a launcher. Just roll up a piece of card into a tube, so the end is the same size as the top of the bottle, and use some tape to stick it down.

3. Take the toothpick and push it through the tube near the bottom. This will stop the sweets falling all the way through the tube before you're ready.

74

4. Don't munch on the sweets yet – you still need them. Now load the launcher with sweets.

5. Open the bottle and put the launcher over it.

6. This is where you need to move quickly. Pull the toothpick out, let the sweets drop, then grab the launcher.

7. Crikey! Watch the fizz fly.

RATINGS

Difficulty

♨♨ ♨♨ ♨♨ ♨♨ ♨♨

Dropping the sweets in is easy; making sure you get out the way is a bit trickier.

Messy

♨♨ ♨♨ ♨♨ ♨♨ ♨♨

This is really messy. Only do this outdoors and use a diet drink because without the sugar it's less sticky. If you can't go outside for some reason, you could try this in the bath, but ask permission first.

Grown-up helper

♨♨ ♨♨ ♨♨ ♨♨ ♨♨

Only to help tidy up afterwards.

Time ⏱

This should take you about **10 minutes**.

What's happening?

We're not entirely sure how this works. It's most likely a combination of two things: a chemical reaction and a physical reaction. It could be the coating on the mint reacting with chemicals within the drink, causing it to fizz up. Or it could be that when you drop the sweets in the drink, the sweets dissolve really quickly and break the surface tension so that the bubbles in the drink can expand more easily and produce more bubbles. The truth is, we can't be sure. So it's up to you to research it and experiment with different types of sweets or maybe even things like salt and sugar. See what works and what doesn't and then see if you can come up with a theory. This could be your opportunity to make your name as a scientist or at least make a mess.

Chromatography

Ink is ink. Do you think? Three black pens: how can you tell them apart? We can, and you can too once you've done this experiment. It can be quite useful, especially if you want to be a spy or detective or if you happen to be someone who's really nosy and likes to know other people's business and who's sending things to other people like a letter about a girl you like and you didn't want the other Punk Scientists knowing and then they did this experiment and found out and told loads of people, which was really embarrassing . . . not that that happened.

Why do chemists have such good breath?

Because they like experi-mints.

Let's get started.

You'll need:

- 3 sheets of blotting paper
- 3 different black water-soluble pens
- A bowl of water
- A washing line

H_2O

CO_2

1. We Punk Scientists like to draw pictures full of colour.

2. These black pens can be full of colour too. Write the same message with each pen on different pieces of blotting paper.

3. Wet the paper and fold one edge to hang it on a washing line to watch the ink run.

4. The inks might look the same colour, but they are actually made up of several different colours.

What's happening?

If you think all ink is the same, you're wrong. Even pens that appear to be of the same colour can be made up of different pigments. Pigments in ink are several different colours that are mixed together to create a solid colour – in this case, black.

This is quite a useful process if you want to take up forensic work. You can trace which pen someone used to write a letter by breaking the ink down in this way.

FACT

Have you ever heard of the Nobel Prize? There isn't just one; there are several prizes ranging over a few subjects, but we tend to associate them with science. The man these prizes are named after was called, guess what! No, not Mr Prize – he was Alfred Nobel, who became famous for inventing dynamite. He was a Swedish scientist who died at the end of the nineteenth century (no, he didn't blow himself up!). Dynamite was important because blowing things up was a bit dodgy at the time and the invention of dynamite made it a bit safer, if blowing things up can ever be safe.

RATINGS

Difficulty

Straightforward, as long as you hang the paper up quickly.

Messy

Be careful not to get covered in ink.

Grown-up helper

You've got this one covered.

Time 🕐

This should take you about **10** to **15 minutes**.

Acid v Alkali

DO THIS AT TRY HOME!

Acids and alkalis don't get on. They're like Dan and washing. To prove this let's see what happens when you mix them together.

Let's get started . . .

RATINGS

Difficulty

Putting stuff in a bag. It's easy.

Messy

Use too much and it'll gunk out all over the place.

Grown-up helper

Only to help tidy up afterwards.

Time 🕐

This should take you about **5 minutes.**

You'll need:
- Some vinegar (30 to 50ml)
- Some bicarbonate of soda (use 3 or 4 heaped tablespoons)
- A plastic resealable freezer bag

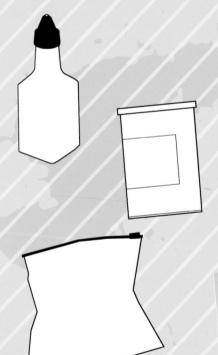

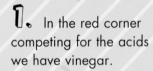

1. In the red corner competing for the acids we have vinegar.

2. In the blue corner competing for the alkalis we have bicarbonate of soda.

3. Put the bicarbonate of soda and vinegar into a resealable freezer bag. Close the bag.

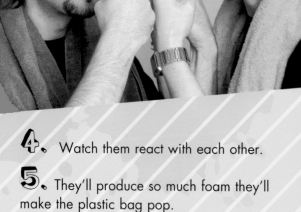

4. Watch them react with each other.

5. They'll produce so much foam they'll make the plastic bag pop.

6. And the winner is neutral.

What's happening?

We use the pH scale to measure what's an acid and an alkali. It runs from 0 to 14. Anything below 7 is an acid and anything above 7 is an alkali. Anything that is bang on 7 is called neutral and is neither acidic nor alkaline.

e.g.

12.5	Bleach
About 9	Soap
7	Water
3	Vinegar
1.5	Stomach acid

Vinegar is quite a weak acid and bicarbonate of soda is quite a weak alkali. But by mixing them together we still get a reaction, an endothermic reaction (one that consumes heat). This produces carbon dioxide, which is what makes the bag expand; we're also left with water. You can try this with a water balloon if you want; it's just a bit more tricky.

FACT

People often think that alchemy is just about crazy people trying to turn lead into gold, creating potions that will cure all illnesses and to increase their own knowledge using the philosophers' stone (not the one from Harry Potter). There was more to it. The experiments and discoveries of alchemists have led us to what we know as chemistry today. You might say that alchemists were the first chemists.

Why shouldn't you ignore chemicals?
Because they like a reaction.

Liquid Layers

We've got an admission to make to you: sometimes there are cross words at Punk Science HQ and I don't mean the type that come in newspapers. We argue and then we have to stay away from each other. Eventually though we kiss and make up, except without the kissing. None of this is important though, because this next experiment shows you what happens when things really don't want to mix.

Let's make some liquid layers.

You'll need:

- A clear container (capacity: 1 litre)
- 330ml oil
- 330ml water
- 330ml honey

1. Carefully pour the honey into your container. You'll need to fill it about one-third full.

2. Now pour the water in as the middle layer.

RATINGS

Difficulty
⚖ ⚖ ⚖ ⚖ ⚖

If you can't do a little pour, you are a little poor.

Messy
⚖ ⚖ ⚖ ⚖ ⚖

It can spill over the sides if you're not careful.

Grown-up helper
⚖ ⚖ ⚖ ⚖ ⚖

Only to help tidy up afterwards.

Time ⏱

This should take you about **5 minutes**.

3. Finally the oil goes in on top.

4. The liquids won't mix and they'll stay in their separate layers.

FACT

Alexander Fleming wasn't a dirty man but he was a bit messy. But in this case being messy was good, because Fleming accidentally left out one of his Petri dishes one day and some bacteria grew on it. On closer inspection of the antibacterial qualities of this special growth, he realized he'd discovered penicillin, which was later transformed into an important medicine. So being messy can be OK.

What's happening?

If you can seal the top of your container, try shaking it up. You'll see that even after a good shake eventually the layers will return. This happens because the liquids have different densities. In this case honey is the most dense so it sinks to the bottom, followed by water and the least dense is oil. That's why if an oil tanker has a leak the oil floats on the surface of the sea. You can try out different liquids to see what they do and how many layers you can get.

1907

First synthetic plastic –
Bakelite – is invented. Nearly
everything is made of plastic
these days – even we are.
Or at least Brad's hair is

Timeline

1897

Marie Curie discovers radium.
You would think this was
a pretty smart move, but
what wasn't a smart move
was keeping radium in her
pocket. She died of radiation
poisoning

1869

Mendeleev publishes his
first version of the periodic
table. That's all the elements
that had been discovered –
and a few that hadn't – all
in groups and everything in
a big shiny table

1867

Joseph Lister
starts the use of
antiseptic surgery.
Yeah, germs, take
some of this!

Way back

5 billion years ago the sun formed. Well, it's made of hydrogen and helium – they're elements so it counts as chemistry

start here

Quite far back

Discovery of fire . . . err about 400,000 years ago. We don't really know

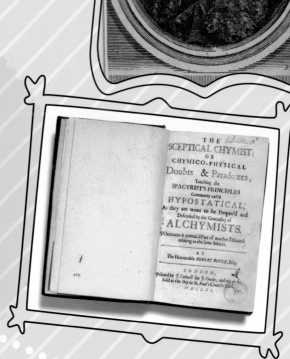

1661

Robert Boyle's *The Sceptical Chemist* is published – one of the first books about chemistry. If you're wondering what he was sceptical about, he didn't just want to take people's word for why something happened – he wanted to prove it using experiments. A bit like you, with the experiments in this book

1864

Louis Pasteur proves disease is caused by germs. Those nasty little germs . . .

83

Do Try the Quiz

So you think you're pretty clever just because you've made it all the way to the back of the book. How do we know we can trust you? How do we know that you haven't just skipped to the end to find out who did it . . . Well, the joke is on you because that only happens in crime novels and this is an experiment book and if you were expecting a culprit to be named you've got snot for brains and if you've got snot for brains don't sneeze whatever you do, otherwise you'll be completely brainless, like Brad.

Just to make sure, we devised a fiendishly clever quiz for you to do as proof you've completed the book.

1.
Look carefully at the pictures of the Punk Scientists. Who would win the competition for biggest nose?

2.
On page 53 how many books can you see?

3.
What country did Alcock and Brown's biplane crash in?

4.
In what year did Russia put the first person in space?

5.
What musical instrument does Jon play?

6.
In the picture on page 11, how many paper clips can you actually see attached to the hot-air balloon?

7.
Somewhere in the Energy chapter we said we'd put something rather odd on our cornflakes. What was it?

8.
What speed did Robert Stephenson's steam engine reach in 1829?

9.
What did we use the electro-magnet to pick up?

10.
Who or what are volts named after?

11.
Who is hiding underneath a sheet in the Light & Sound chapter?

84

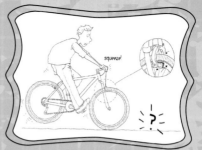

16.
From top to bottom, what order are the liquid layers in?

17.
How many people can talk on the string mobile phone at any one time?

18.
What is the weight of the medicine ball used in the Flight & Space chapter?

19.
What animal is nearly run over by a bicycle in the Forces chapter?

20.
What is the more scientific and sensible name for power that comes from burning poo?

12.
What colour pen is being used in the colour wheel?

13.
Which two different types of fruit juice are used in the periscope experiment?

14.
Who patented the first lightbulb, in 1878?

15.
What famous equation is written on the pieces of paper in the Chemistry chapter?

OK, you can relax now, there are no more questions. Unless of course you want more questions, in which case we could tell you where to find some more. But you'd have to make it worth our while – maybe you could send us some ice cream. No, that would melt. Cake! Send us cake and we'll tell you where to find another quiz. We trust you so we'll tell now, secure in the knowledge you will send a delicious baked item and not just go to **www. sciencemuseum.org. uk/trythis**, do the quiz and forget about us and our need for cake.

HOW DID YOU SCORE?

15–20
You are a true genius.

10–15
Not bad, but were you paying enough attention? If the answer is no, then you're probably not even reading this bit, which is OK because you didn't miss anything special.

5–10
Go back and try again and see if you can do better. That's if you have the rest of the book and didn't just find this quiz page in a ditch, which might account for your score.

0–5
Are you a member of the Punk Science team?

Answers

1. Brad by a nose
2. 33
3. Ireland
4. 1961
5. He can't play any musical instruments – he can't even clap
6. 1, but there is another still in Jon's hand
7. Gravy
8. 29 miles per hour
9. Paper clips
10. Alessandro Volta
11. Dan
12. Green
13. Apple and orange
14. Joseph Swan
15. $E = MC^2$
16. Oil, water, honey
17. One. There might be two people using it but it only works when one person is talking and the other is listening. Otherwise you won't hear anything
18. 3 kg
19. A mouse
20. Biomass

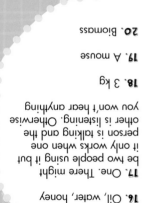

Glossary

A

absorb To take in or swallow up something, like a sponge absorbs water

acid Something that has a pH value of less than 7. Acids can be things that taste sour, and strong acids can melt through certain materials

alchemy An early form of chemistry, usually associated with turning lead into gold

alkali Something that has a pH value above 7

atom The smallest part of an element, consisting of a nucleus orbited by electrons, that still has the chemical properties of the element

attract/attraction To pull something closer, like magnets attract metal

B

Bernoulli Daniel Bernoulli, the 17th-century Swiss scientist who showed that air pressure goes down when air speeds up

billion A thousand million, but it used to mean a million million

biplane An early type of aeroplane that has two sets of wings, one set above the other

biomass Biological matter, usually plants or poo used for burning as fuel

buoyancy The upward force from a liquid that makes things float

C

Celsius A temperature scale named for Anders Celsius in which freezing water is zero and boiling water is 100

charge In electricity you either get positive or negative charges

chromatography

chromatography A technique used to separate the parts of liquids or gases

coil A spiral or series of loops, like in a spring

compass A device used to show magnetic north to help to find the direction you want to go

compounds A substance that consists of two or more elements

compressed/compression To squeeze, press or push something

copper A reddish-brown metal that is a good electrical conductor

CO₂ the symbol for carbon dioxide, which contains one carbon atom and two oxygen atoms

D

decibels A unit for the measurement of sound

density How tightly packed something is

diagram A technical drawing, often used to help explain something

DNA Deoxyribonucleic acid – a very large molecule shaped like a spiral staircase that carries genetic information that determines characteristics such as eye and hair colour

domains Tiny magnets that are in ferrous metals like iron, they tend to point in all different directions cancelling each other out, but get them to point in the same direction and that piece of metal will become magnetic

drag A force resisting the movement of an object

dynamite A type of explosive

E

Einstein Albert Einstein, the physicist who first theorized that matter and energy are the same thing and that time and space are the same thing

economist A person who studies how resources, goods and services are distributed in a society

electromagnet A device that converts electrical energy into a magnetic field; a magnet that can be turned on or off

electromagnetic waves Energy which travels through space, including X-rays, radio waves, light waves, microwaves, infrared radiation, ultraviolet radiation and gamma rays

electron A subatomic particle with a negative electric charge

element A substance that only has one type of atom in it – like oxygen and unlike carbon dioxide which has two types of atoms in it

endothermic A reaction that absorbs heat

exothermic A reaction that produces heat

experiment A test or series of tests carried out in order to find answers

F

float Being freely suspended in a liquid or gas

forces Something that exerts a push or a pull on an object

friction A force that slows things down, usually when two or more objects rub together

fusion The process of combining atomic nuclei that releases enormous amounts of energy

G

gas The state of a substance after a solid and a liquid, where the atoms that make up the substance move around quickly and all over the place

generate To produce or make something, such as electricity

geologist Someone who studies the earth and rocks

glider A heavier-than-air craft that flies without an engine

gravity The force that pulls all things with a mass towards each other

Galileo An Italian astronomer and physicist

H

harness To use and control the energy of something

heat A type of energy indicated through temperature

helicopter A flying machine with powered rotor blades

helium A type of gas that is lighter than air

Hertz A German physicist who studied electromagnetic forces

hovercraft A vehicle that moves on a cushion of air

hydrogen A chemical element that is normally a gas or part of water

hydro-power Power derived from moving water

I

ice Solid state of water

J

jet A type of aircraft that uses gas turbine engines, usually pretty quick

joules A unit used to measure work. In this case work doesn't mean where you go to do your job, it's actually a term for the amount of energy used to do something, like the energy you used to lift up this book

K

kerosene A type of fuel used in planes and burned for heat

kinetic Movement energy

L

LED Light-emitting diode

lift The force that helps things fly

lightning An electric discharge occurring between clouds or between a cloud and the earth

M

magnetic field The area of force surrounding a magnet

magnetic pole Either the north or south end of a magnet or of the earth

magnetism The force of attraction that magnets have

mass How much of something there is

molecules The combination of the elements that make up a compound

movement a change of position

N

NASA National Aeronautics and Space Administration (USA)

nuclear Referring to atomic nuclei, as in nuclear energy

neutral Neither acidic nor alkaline, having a pH of 7

neutrons Particles in the nucleus of an atom

O

oxygen An element that is part of the air we breathe

P

particles A really tiny piece of something

periscope An optical device that uses mirrors so you can see things indirectly

perspex A type of plastic

philosopher A person who studies how we should behave, whether things exist, how we know what we know and how to prove things

photovoltaic Converting light energy directly into electricity

physical reaction A reaction where the substance changes but not into another substance, so when water becomes ice it's the same thing just in a different state, whereas a chemical reaction is like when you add something to the water to make it into something else

pigments Elements of a colour

plane A type of aircraft

polymer A compound that has a structure made up of long molecules in chains

polystyrene A type of synthetic material used in packing

power A measurement of work per unit time

pressure The exertion of force on something

prism A transparent object that separates white (normal) light into its component colours

propellers A device that converts rotating motion into thrust as on an airplane or ship

Proton A positively charged particle found in the nucleus of an atom (see neutron)

R

radio An electronic device used to listen to music and sometimes dull people talking

radio wave A type of electromagnetic wave that transports the music and dull people talking that we listen to

reaction A response or force that is equal and opposite to another force

relativity According to Galileo, relativity shows that the laws of physics remain the same no matter where you are

reflection The result of waves bouncing off a surface, as in light waves hitting a mirror

S

signal To receive or send a message in some shape or form

sink The opposite of floating

solar sail A theoretical device similar to a wind sail that catches solar radiation to propel a ship. One day a solar sail might power a spacecraft

soluble Something that is easily dissolved, usually in water

space–time A way of describing the universe in which there are four dimensions: three of space and one of time; it is associated with Einstein's theories

static electricity The build-up of electrical potential (charge) in a non-conducting material, often released as an arc when a conductor is brought close

streamlined Usually an object that has reduced resistance to air or a fluid

sun Big hot thing in the sky

T

telescope A device that uses lenses to make distant objects appear closer

temperature How cold or hot something is

transfer To change or move from one thing to another

turbine A machine that transfers energy, often into electricity using large rotors

U

upthrust The upward force that helps things float

V

vibrate To shake or move something back and forth repeatedly

volt A measurement of electrical potential

W

wavelength The distance between the crest or trough of one wave and the next

wing Either on a bird or a plane to help them fly

wire Strands of metal used to pass electricity through

weight How heavy something is

Z

zinc A type of metal

Also available from Macmillan Children's Books in association with the Science Museum

Why Is Snot Green?

And other extremely important questions (and answers) from the Science Museum

Glenn Murphy

978-0-330-44852-9   £5.99

Why is snot green? Do spiders have ears? Do rabbits fart? How big is Space?

Find out the answers to these and an awful lot of other brilliant questions in this funny and informative book.

Stuff Tha[t] Scares You[r] Pants Off[!]

The Science Museu[m] Book of Scary Thing[s] (and ways to avoid the[m])

Glenn Murph[y]

978-0-330-47724-6   £4.9[9]

What scares you most? Spiders or shark[s] Ghosts or aliens? Dentists or darkness[?]

This amazing book takes apart your deepes[t] darkest fears. With a bit of biology and a sp[?] of psychology you'll learn everything there is [to] know about the stuff that scares your pants o[ff]

Once you have read this book, you will be ab[le] to look terror in the eye and make it run awa[y] whimpering. You might even want to chang[e] your middle name to 'dange[r]'

How Loud Can You Burp?

And other extremely important questions (and answers) from the Science Museum

Glenn Murphy

978-0-330-45409-4   £5.99

How loud can you burp? What are clouds for? Why don't big metal ships sink? Why is water wet, and is there anything wetter than water? Could we use animal poo to generate electricity?

This is a wonderfully funny and informative book which helps us take a fresh look at the world (and universe) we live in, with no boring bits and an abundance of fascinating facts.